A BEAUTIFUL NAME

FOR A GIRL

A BEAUTIFUL NAME FOR A GIRL

KIRSTEN KASCHOCK

AHSAHTA PRESS
BOISE, IDAHO / 2011

Ahsahta Press, Boise State University
Boise, Idaho 83725-1525
http://ahsahtapress.boisestate.edu
http://ahsahtapress.boisestate.edu/books/kaschock/kaschock.htm

Library of Congress Cataloging-in-Publication Data

Kaschock, Kirsten.
A beautiful name for a girl / Kirsten Kaschock.
    p. cm. -- (The new series ; #38)
ISBN-13: 978-1-934103-17-3 (pbk. : alk. paper)
ISBN-10: 1-934103-17-9 (pbk. : alk. paper)
I. Title.
PS3611.A785B43 2011
811'.6—DC22

                              2010032769

ACKNOWLEDGMENTS

The following poems have been published or accepted for publication in the following journals (although sometimes in different versions under different titles): *American Letters & Commentary*: "Assemblage," "O Dearest, Dearest B."; *Barrow Street*: "Laundryroom, a Prayer Cycle"; *Blue Mesa Review*: "Orphanage: A Pastoral"; *Chibbachibba*: a small section of "Snuff Ballet (a Monologue for 2, 3, or 7)"; *Court Green*: "Eight Rooms In," "Maiden Mead"; *The Diagram*: "Houdini dies. I teach his obituary."; *Denver Quarterly*: "Sold Into Performance"; *Effing Magazine*: "Writing Spider"; *Euphony*: "In the Atlas of Birds"; *Gulf Coast*: "Man-Made"; *GutCult*: "Inertia Quartet"; *How2*: "The 18 Gates of Sage"; *La Petite Zine*: "Gallery of the Daughter," "Tips from Your Salvation," "Positional"; *LIT*: "Marriage(2)," a small section of "Snuff Ballet (a Monologue for 2, 3, or 7)"; *Melic Review*: "Kept: a Thimbleful of Ache," "Dutiful, the Sister"; *No Tell Motel*: "Bad Night, Bad," "Jostling, a Consolation," "Marlene Dietrich at 70 Had Legs that Shot to Heaven," "She will say *it's not personal* and she will *it's over*"; *Octopus*: "How Noun," "Baby Names—Girl F"; *Pleiades*: "The Bride Machine"; *Spinning Jenny*: "Daughter Song"; *Tarpaulin Sky*: "Marriage(1)," "Deposition"; *Volt*: "Old Doll Body"

I would like to thank the following people (who may or may not be aware of the things-they-have-done): Jed Rasula, Judith Cofer, Reginald McKnight, Claudia Rankine, Alexander Kaschock, Taryn Kaschock, Mary Oliveira, Misha Kaschock, Ann & Alex Kaschock, Maureen Smith, Michael Rioux, Sarah Yake, Mark Young, Sîan Griffiths, John Woods, Sabrina Orah Mark, Heather Matesich, Mark Leidner, Danielle Pafunda, Kristen Iskandrian, Lara Glenum, Johannes Göransson, Becca Waugh, Tina Lee-Godbey, Sung-Ji Schmidt, Patrick Lawler, Danny Marenda, Simon, Bishop, and Koen.

for Rat and Maybe and Mo,
for Maya and Nan and Jodie

CONTENTS

1

I have no arms or legs.
I'm all one skin like a fish…
—*Anne Sexton*

ASSEMBLAGE

This is the house Jane built.

Jane begins by standing. Once, this was
Jane finding Jane. Jane avows
a new architecture, its velocity out
rather than up—the foundation in flowers.

First, a field

A making ready. Then, in the foreground—
                                 relevance.
Jane's erection of self: a marker
indicating horizon. *Look* her body in the middle
of all things is saying *what was already here*
Not a greedy Jane. A Jane acknowledging.

Meadow first, then—a positioning of Jane
as verticality. As perpendicular to.
Jane, stated.
                 But also Jane
is temporal
cleft: *a Jane streaming out of the field*

No longer field, Jane becomes
a thing requiring.

Jane whole unto. Jane isolate.

Order Jane learning *is like a god and like a god punitive*

Jane seeking to embrace field is straining
Jane, incapable.

                    —but now I am
in a unique position to feel pain this is distinct
insistent Jane, Jane fraught *I have*
more space for pain Above the primordial
flowering of was, a shimmer.
In its wake—structure: Jane is.

It is less space.

This is the house Jane built by being the house
Jane built by being. This is not
the good pain—pain
Jane stood to feel *in origin of Jane*

Instead, this is pain of lean-to—
uncontaining. Mere stay
against exposure. This is all is left
a Jane. This is enough.

The machine is visible only at sunset, at the cusp.

The machine is entirely of lace—you can't hear it?

That's something wrong with you.

It is simple as blood on an apple.

The machine is capable of fornication but *chooses* wither.

The machine has never been caught whistling, never exhibited caprice, never
  smoldered.

It holds to the stalk.

A million tockings from other timepieces will not jar our machine loose.

The machine will stay, or the machine will fetch.

Above all else, the machine desires to please.

Organize a dinner party, and the machine will offer up her vagina.

Here, this is not unlike that.

The machine is aware that the machine is a replacement.

The machine as clone of the other.

The other had an actual voice. The other opened with intent, and closed
  unexpectedly.

The machine hopes you will eventually forget the subtle differences in texture.

In this economy, after all, what is lost can be re-constituted.

It is known.

In the atlas of birds it is written: "warblers
are born with eyes embedded deep
within their throats; they quickly come
to addiction—admiring the sight
of their own song, they revise it only
slightly, yet relentlessly repeat
the uninspired variations." The book
also comments at length on larger birds.
"The backward knees of the ostrich,"
the atlas tells, "propel the animal
across inhospitable grasslands
at over thirty miles per hour." Mistakes are,
as often as not, improvements (so says
the book) could one ignore aesthetic
concerns—ostriches being "a species
whose countenance prohibits such god-like
acts as flight." The atlas calls the beat
of a hummingbird heart "a quickening
so rapid the blood flows in a continuous
stream, much like florescence." Could I
be the light in a bird's veins, the vain
eye in its throat, the glittering speed
that compensates its hideous perversion—
I would allow certain inaccuracies
reported of me. I am not, I have
not, these qualities. Regardless,
I prefer an uncelebrated life, absent
from the books of category, avoiding
the fact I am—faulty, and
deviant as any bird—reducible miracle.

HOUDINI DIES. I TEACH HIS OBITUARY.

I.

famous as a defier
an exposer of here this afternoon spiritualism

He relates to my own domesticity in the following manner:

2.

underwent two operations.
due to the second
a newly discovered chapter of accidents
ended fatally for thousands.

> Outside, the last bite
> of fall. Yellow leaves wince.

Nearing end of semester One, trimester Two.

to be cheating the very jaws of October
on the opening night

> Only I only mention trees—magicians—
> directing away from my body
> to say   this is not
> not about me.

> Traps, trees, locusts—
> their thorned vines
> strangling them with protection.

I missed a class in September.
Left an assignment: write meaningfully about nature.

3.

his engagement apparatus—
his "water torture cell"—overturned.
struck him on the audience.

> About this:
> how small my world is—and whether or not
> it is small in the right ways.

Narrow your subject. Limit your thesis. This is not arguable.

then, completed his performance—
afterward the injured fractured
Houdini [would] discontinue,
however, not miss a show.

> Spoons, cups: these are too small.
> Window: again, too.

Bouts of nausea did not keep me from 8AM classes.
I was not about to die. Remember—he fit through anything.

his company went to a Schenectady called pain.

If one leaf is a grove, a glass
of ice water
lake—you may be a poet.
For a woman, make metaphors
larger—prison might stretch
into city. Other women must
believe in your confinement. To be
a woman is after all what?

A: To give. (3 out of 5 points… full sentences. Please.)

4.

his removal keen and alert.
the patient, combined with stamina, did much
to prolong the direct cause of Houdini's system of death.

One day, my students looked through me.

> They heard my blood creep
> and stall, pressure
> too low. Asked was I sick.

this is particularly virulent.

How should I know that? May I ask them it now?
Now they've forgotten me over sour beer, their lovers' stomachs, coffee?

the body was born on March 24, 1874.

> It was pity. My black
> periphery was showing. They never
> imagine how often I
> teeter at the edge of the language
> I comb out of them like lice.

5.

his name, the son of a rabbi.

Pregnant.

I tell them.

6.

even before opening his first kitchen closet, it is certain
he showed fluidity as a "flight artist."

>In the shower, yellow-white tears trail
>off purpled aureoles: a dark factory
>of thin sweet pus—

Some see me as captor. Holding their future hostage.
Or puppet to some theater company, deserving of late work,
unsupported claims. I am not, after all, reality.

at the age of 9 joined a trapeze.

>I am—
>to drop the child from the sack that it may
>sun itself, eat.

the first were bound inside themselves,
any bonds inspired Houdini somewhat.

The female students wonder passively about my age, marital status, contagion.

>Foals open a mare stark
>minutes before they walk.
>Mare remains, must,
>standing.

I think   I have had enough with children.

7.

similarly, in the middle of handcuffs
the taunt: "If I go much longer—you will stay
on the usual hands."

       Please, I am begging—
       do not attempt your own release.
       This body should not be
       fled. Is not fire.

Anymore. I do not know what I am thinking.

8.

his long series of shackles (70,000)
returned him broken from self-assassination.

> There have been other mothers—
> ones who dipped sudden, strange hands and lips
> into the red, let their eyes
> grow
>
> > too bright to take.

Can my students comprehend the complexities
of *buried alive*? To emerge as something genius—
or not emerge, but perhaps, then—do no harm?
        No—
they want an A.

skyscraper strait-jacket, from which
to the applause of the boat or bridge into a river,
by drowning or suffocation, a minute
or so, then a free man—vigorously.

Twenty-two eighteen-year olds have not learned to string between them
the tightrope of one living sentence.
Potential: to throw myself down a flight of stairs.

9.

in his early days
he used to seance: "I had gone around
the inscriptions and acquired a time
of gradually." an exclaiming:
"throat is a body with shrieks"

    Two cities. Pain, emergence.
    I will suffer   briefly
    as cocoon, manacle—
    will lose a life into the air.

They begin to ask—will I cancel the last paper, grade on what's been done?
And what have you created?   This, without irony.

for thirty-three years Houdini
was anxious to believe
hundreds (fourteen of those
had ever counted)

Write your own obituary: write it about someone you admire.

II.

he risked his grave:
it gave him the first thrill of the irretrievable—
to waste a fraction of air
when every fraction was loose about his body
Houdini said   "I began to fail [it was]
yet another mistake"

that I am   a vessel   useless   essential   a vessel

that I   am   am not   a teacher

that I have   carried hatred beside a child

that I do not write   *my child*

that I am not   stronger   will not   get   stronger

that this   after all   after everything   is irreversible

12.

Houdini (describing the most narrow):
        my self-possession left me. it was a blinding blessing—chalky, wild-eyed—
        out of a shallow plot—my friends tell me I was a perfect
        imitation of rising.

I will breathe it only once

        I am also: perfect
                              imitation

as soon as you can—

                              escape

MAN-MADE

for Mitchell Baker

An airplane is a terrible thing.
It has a terrible height.
Airplanes are moveable Babels, and I
and you, and everyone
know not to reach that way for God, up—
that a god
is a small thing and comes by being quiet.
An airplane is also steel, and steel
is terrible. And Pittsburgh a terrible place
because of the steel. We should
not move there. If we do not move at all
a god may come, by not flying.
Not by wings by quiet
a trembling that begins no war
may work itself from underneath
skin or earth, a warmth
may bloom in the mouth like an alcohol
not at all like alcohol. This is how a god
would begin in you, or anyone
or me. Not blown
across an ocean, or pumped out of depths
slick and flammable. Aren't gods
what happen in us
when we listen for gods?
I do not think a god enlists machines
for proof. And gods do not favor
the way birds move
over the flight of dolphins.
It is a terrible thing for you
to think so.

FABLE   the one you think would go on, but circles back, her daily calls almost a nuisance—wasn't she supposed to do something *special*?

FAYE   a liar. she will have nine lives, each a different color red

FELL   this one, after reading in her own handwriting too many times her own name, goes down the well

FENDI   won't stop herself, will hit a series of dead-end romances, end up on the couch with a therapist, skirt hiked, hubcaps flashing

FIGARO   talented, perhaps—so what?

FILO   flaky but kind, air coated in butter. this one will have your number, never visit, float through LSD episodes like skin cells in an attic, neglect a mind for math, take showers that run cheap motels out of hot water

FINK   you don't name a babygirl Fink

FLAIL   the dutiful daughter never succeeding, everyone eventually succumbing to cancer and having their insides scoured out with Comet

FOLLY   an Xmas child with bows, wrapped tighter than a heart. a three-year old with a pout sickos cream for

FOMENT   a solid engine of girl—writes thank-yous, is probably going to marry her father, has one recurrent rape fantasy involving a church

FOOT   a child in the mouth

FRAN   for your great-grandmother, her mugs of scotch and milk, white ghosts, cellophane in the freezer—you wooed her dying for the brooch you wanted, an opal—this girl, also, a cursed stone

FRIDAY   stays at home weekends organizing the refrigerator

FURY   a name for a girl with charming hair. you could never have this one, not with your coloring

FYNE   what you eventually name her—resigned to predicating her ruin

The boy loves trucks. His is a world of Vrrum. I am most comfortable sitting behind the tall grass wondering if the lions are going to eat my mother. The boy gestures. Come closer, he says. Come closer to the big wheels. Of everything, he likes the grill most. His fingers talk open the buttons of my dress. I am more and more willing to unpack the steam trunk where nothing is left but mosquito netting for a blouse. I will not. Instead, there are the insects to feed—for years, I am comprised of a series of small raised white welts. He has come to want something he can take down with his rifle and like a young god fling across the slatted floor of the truck bed. During the same period, I have shrunken to the size of a petri dish.

Mother wanted to make me available to the gypsies. I won't call you
what you are. I wasn't raised to be that type of Friday.
I am good practice for reading cards. I've always won at Go
Fish. I've been the one who hid her numbers best. My favorites
were the standards: *Under your skin, Mood Indigo*
I will. I never sang—I danced but no solos.
I was legs in the frog chorus, at that time strictly
Platonic. You want to put me down as leading lady when I was so much
less. They sell girls to Japan: I love haiku, but am not blond.
I love how nature bounces off of nature democratically. It's like
a motel bed or a trampoline act in Vegas. I've done torch song
in the wings of guerilla theater and other rarely risked venues:
bat mitzvahs, firemen's balls, industrials.
The people you work for, and me, and you too—we like to watch
the represented burn.
                    In the recurrent dream, the fire dream
you ask me to crawl out the window onto the fire ladder.
It's special, you tell me—it's only for second stories.
Looking down, the way I'm never supposed to, I see duct-taped around
each rung a different 8×10 black-and-white glossy.
In order to escape the charred remains of the body through the chest cavity
I am made to climb down faces of the ones left inside. My mother
is there, the other dancers, a few strained vocalists, the doctor. Everyone
but you. Faces of the already and the possibly dead. I keep telling myself
not to worry, that they don't matter. I see their faces only
as the faces of an audience.

Score this, he said handing me the celluloid. The silent short had been lifted from a play. Four women treading water at a buoy or standing outside an organic food store. It had not been successful: too much text—some of it in the original German, the corkscrewing smoke off one of their cigarettes—overstated in black-and-white. I watch it seventeen or eighteen times. I learn their teeth by heart. Each of them makes several attempts to get up and go. That they are talking about malformed lovers, dogs, genocide as metaphor—is dishonest and engaging. But what matters is how they don't end it. I try to score the film with silk, then magnets, then steel cable. I wind brick around platinum for a through-line. I don't get them right. I ask my instructor back in with hither-come eyes and a blond leg out the door. Pleaseplease show me how I've botched it. He watches my version—asks, Where will they go once they manage to dissolve? It shudders me. I decide on an open window, cellophane drifting from an operating table onto the floor. I know this is a trope, but for girls like them, girls unlike me, it is quite good enough.

OLD DOLL BODY

They think mine
a prettypretty blank blank

I could tell them *I am humbly submitting
the same* I could say *here is the same
for your perusal*

Yesterday, it was the same ate through my petticoats
I feared dysplasia, uterine cancer—irrational
fear, symptom of hysteria

I, in fact, fear I will remain the same
even as I ache to send it out to contests
and for test-drives

The same is in my underwear
—has been since I was made

If they knew the same they'd love it like a root
but would want to get away—if the same
were true for them
day in, day out—their fingers would stop
no prettypretty holes down there

They don't know what that's like
everything in and nothing let
inside my forgotten space—cotton

They prize too much response
I prettymuch want it too   rejection, reaction
something that has to do
with something else

keep passing me down they think me
a faithful carrier of the original
embedding   *keep offering the next babygirl*
me   as if I were still just what was given

because even dolls evolve
I give each girl the same
I've given every girl but it is no longer all

I think *this time*
the seams will go but they don't
and I continue with
holding my difference

HOW NOUN

I. THE INVALID

You are my property. This is day one of the longest recovery. This is hour two of the longest day of the infinite recovery. Look at the bed. Look at it. One day soon I will raise myself from the prayers and find a single egg of hope. The egg will be pure. A free market good. An imported preserve. A tulip bulb. An olive. Look at the way my thigh is white. Look at it. Look at the way my thigh is wide. Ocean. This mattress is not the mattress I wanted for our matrimony. That bed was stolen just before the unending night of the disaster. Your mother gave us this one. Your mother nursed you on the bed where we screw. Used to. The mourning is never an honest mourning. Come inside. No, just for a minute. This bed is foreign, a brass vessel. While I've been in it, traveling, the ceiling has lowered itself six inches. Eventually, the ceiling will rest against my forehead like a cool cloth. Please. You'll have to reach out with your sunken palms to push it back. I have wanted and wanted to look up—and have it blue.

The egg is smaller than a hen's egg, and tragic in its virginity. The way the egg will not be cracked is a myth. Many will come. Many from other lands, lands where the sun sets in the southeast and is veined, will come to attempt the egg's opening. It has been rumored that a new god lives inside the egg. A god that looks like a feather. But the egg will not offer itself. The egg has the type of volition that refuses. Nevertheless, many will come. One, especially, will come. She will sit on the egg, giving the egg a mother. She will lend a certain warmth to the egg which has always been colder than frostbite and green-black. After a number of years, the egg will move from absolute zero, attaining temperature. At that moment, the egg will begin to shift internally. Its escape from stasis will prohibit the possibility of any god. The egg sitter will then stand. She will bow a slight but fractious bow, knowing she was somehow involved, and that something has been saved from grace.

The god that looks like a feather has waited over seven millennia to be born. Much can be learned in the time before sowing. Witness the pitch of the horizon frozen between tree branches. Or the subtle differences in serial number. When a god waits, it is because a god does not mind waiting, and the waiting has merit. It is unlike the waiting in an oncologist's office or until the nuptials. When a god waits, it is as in music: a fermata. The subliminal grandeur of a god's birth should happen during a nebula or in the eye beyond the pale. Time, for such-and-such a god, does not move forward nor circle back behind the register for a hidden revolver. It simply pulls to the left. A god adjusts. A god ducks under the boardwalk for an hour with close and fecund purpose. Even when the millennia are quick with the hook-and-eye, even when they swagger, they are fingernail clippings at the water's edge. Senselessly clawing. A god that looks like a feather does not need patience—its being eternal and all.

I have come here to write it from the inside out.

This is a room inside a room, inside six more rooms. I am in the eighth room in. Where it might be safe. There are no windows; that would be a mistake. Windows allow access to the jugular, which isn't wanted.

I have a wife and child. I meant to say husband. I meant to say I am a wife and child. No, mother.

They know I've left them for awhile. Their version of awhile is not mine. I have left them to come here, to be further inside here, and to write a way out.

Pinpointing, by nature, is an act of paranoia. One must assume that others have a tendency to misunderstand. Perhaps they intend to misunderstand. Diabolical has its roots in this.

I should describe the room. If you are in the room, you should recognize it, so that you may develop the desire to get out.

The room is the size of a toilet.

The room has no corners, or if it has corners, they meet in an irregular fashion. The couplings of wall take place in the most remote reaches. The ceiling isn't level. The floor—unidentifiable as floor.

I come here because I know it. I come here at night, or during the day when my son sits in front of the television. He sits right up next to the television, so that the television is large for him. I am farther away, and the television has become less important.

The room is cold. Not as cold as a refrigerator, but lit like that.

When I shut myself in, it is very dim but I can still see. The room gives me certain powers that I may only exhibit within the room itself. That is how the room exhibits its own power. Understand?

When his father comes home, my son jumps up, and the room is punctured. That is why this time I have gone eight rooms in. It will take them much trouble to get to me. I am sorry for that.

The doors are heavier than you might think, and they are filled with water. Once they are shut, that is the end. The ones who have drowned between the rooms press their faces toward the inner chambers.

Here, paper and pens are strictly forbidden, as they can be windows. You must remember at all times to protect the neck and the wrists and the belly.

I smuggled my paper in, carrying it inside my mouth, like an alligator with young. Folded down. Unfolded, the paper was crippled. That did not matter. Here, I can nurse things back to health.

It is a thing I cannot do elsewhere.

DAUGHTER SONG

(1)

Out of a body, the heart.
I wrapped it in red lettuce and sang to it.
I don't know why it was more fall than I was.

The turning of the year
that usually anchored things
was extricating them.

Imagine my fear.

Removal of this, removal of
beauty, infancy.

(2)

Winter. The other word for aging.

Yearly, fewer people make it through January
than other months. On the radio.

I sang to the muscle even as it grew
ashy. The song was continuing pain.

I gave it up like fainting choirboys.
I gave it up like cancer.

I have no control over what comes out of me.

(3)

Bereft of the heart, the body
refused to lullaby. To lie down.

I could not make the body into a doll.
I had to leave it behind in the grass

to break down. While I went off
circling the tender
dying woods with its heart in a leaf.

TIPS FROM YOUR SALVATION

This is my Resurrection Moniker—
the name you must call me in order to be raised,
the list of acts I'd like you to perform.

    Ransom.
    Be efficient, but skimping,
      realize thick hymnals will fill with hieroglyphs.

I do not want you to imagine you will fit into grace easily.

There are bound to be feet. Toes or heels lopped.
Maybe a hacking at the knee, you dromedary.

    The chosen will not be looked at through the eye.

And as I inserted your application just under
razor wire, the chosen may not recognize you.
Hearing the whistle

    jump the nearest back and grab fitfully, shirt.

Your woman will make it to the border, even with
the weight of you and the children.
You will not have known this about her.

    I am your woman. You have not known.

Breakfast is clay ground to porridge
by mastication. I can do this for you, have done.
Now you must do something.

Rampage. Brief, holistic wars.
38-aught-6. Iota of crouch.
Field-plate, arachnid, campfire.

This begins our code. Once you break it, the surf will rise.
And me all around your ankles—salted and desultory.

LAUNDRYROOM, A PRAYER CYCLE

1. *sort*

> if I can come to quiet
> then
>
> I will have what I am not supposed
> to have, have meaning: clutch, have
> meaning: having wanted when want
> is for bad
>
> quiet is the latch
> to the box locked with god

2. *warm-cold*

> if I can come to quiet
>
> when worlds around me, three spun
> men—planets each pulley
> wheel and rope mandalas strangling
> me with a love-like
> need
>
> > —then god

3. *wash*

> yet amid such I cannot god
> I ground myself
> in them, instead, gravities

and suspended, webbed dew
is like quiet
but is not quiet

4. *rinse*

it will be decades, deaths
downhills of grief, goose quilt and numb
pinion—the heroin of over

before god will displace this terrifying hold
this keep and keep and keep

5. *spin*

so near to oubliette
why does it matter where I am losing my

self, to whom? I know
it is—but why is quiet a way? please god

let battle be another

But this is not that story.
We were moving, with cardboard boxes.
We could not get at it with a broom, but
there was a bird dying for three days
in the chimney. I called the landlord, he said
the bird is already dead. The bird was not
already. The bird was not dead. The bird
spent three days dying. I was finished with school
in the house for three days packing with Led
Zeppelin because of the loud. So there was that,
the three-year old, the infant, me and drowning
chimney sounds: furious, then—
pointless. It was three days, each with a little
less bird, and a fourth day with nothing.
And we left after that day. We left the day after
the nothing day—packing done
bird dead.
                    I will always
hate Syracuse. We will never be friends.

MARLENE DIETRICH AT 70 HAD LEGS THAT SHOT TO HEAVEN

Her eyes at 70 said, I've never cared at all.

When she sang, it was
to dance. She was consummate.

Practice, practice, and being paid to die. She had
all I've ever wanted.

Her gestapo posture in Vegas, the night
I was born. I saw it all on A&E.

She sang about spring that night and it was about death.
She smiled, and death.

She tucked a curl of an obvious wig back
into place and it was death.

I was born on the last gasp of her glittering
shroud, although she didn't die until she was 90.

She was motionless when she danced it in Vegas
the night of my birth. Her hands clasped behind her.

To dance the death dance, to wrap
the black shawl

around my waist, twirl, shoulders, twirl, face
is all I have ever been given to want.

In a few turns death rises
to make beauty. *Look*— they say

See the pale face, the blood-weary
lips seeking blue.

I will be her with the silk fringe on the edge
of edge. Heel, toe.

Stomp. Pull.   Drag.   Fall
and rise.

They will ask— *How*
many times is it possible to rise?

Elbows turned out, palms to ceiling
and balanced on each painful finger—particular death.

Make no mistake, she is a witch—
they will say— *see how she dances.*

Marlene let it be filmed. I will not
let it be filmed.

I will not hand over this dance to another
girl, born to it—

bloody come and strangling to this world.

2

pas de deux—forced to
partner herself
woman is: crowd scene

SNUFF BALLET (A MONOLOGUE FOR 2, 3, OR 7)

[six faces. covening over a black table. hair back-slicked. mouths dark. open voltages.
a hand sweeps. a cross. one end to another. one end to another]

Why a one-woman show? Tell us—is this performance art?

Can it be somehow about surgery?

How will the audience sit through two hours of her?

Can the stage support rain? Can there be a flood? Can she be both ante and post-diluvian?

Can she contain that many animals?

Will it be too gestural? Totemic? Psychoanalytical?

Who will fund it?

How will you find a dancer with that type of stamina? Will you drug her?

Can it be somehow about surgery?

Have you considered Hiroshima?

Does that make you feel like a man? Enough like?

Is she barefoot? What about lifts? There won't be any… will that restrict you?

Costume changes. None again… will that restrict you?

What restricts you? Is that what this is about?

Will the critics label it a dissertation? Will you be offended?

Can you be offended? Is that your intention?

Where is the movement coming from? Will it be pedestrian, or stylized?

When was the last time you had sex?

And whom was that with?

Why do you think there are no maternal characters in your ballet?

Does our calling it a ballet offend you? Will you take up the term to prove that it didn't?

Why no gods? Fathers? Why no lovers? Why only one woman?

Might she be schizophrenic?

Is she promiscuous? How would you show that, with no other dancers?

If she dry humps the stage, will that be seen as masturbation or possession?

Can she contain that many animals?

Is it about the bible in the end? We read it out of love. Why did you read it?

Is she supposed to be Jesus?

Can she swim?

Why so unrelenting? Whom are you refusing peace? Why are you so angry?

You do realize you will alienate half your audience?

Will she wear a veil?

Why call yourself an abstract expressionist? Why not a Marxist? Why modern dance?

This isn't about communicating, is it?

Can it be somehow about surgery?

Why, do you think, you haven't yet learned to bleed by yourself?

[lights out. a square. spotlight fixes a woman in. discomfort. blush-colored dress. as she speaks. she twists.]

I refuse you the glory. You may think your questions reveal; in truth, they diffract. These are confetti aspersions. You think you are wry and acrylic. I've been in parades. I've twirled. Two hours of tossing and which hurts more, shoulder or ankles? And how cold the body—despite fire batons. I've been very cold. From the sockets. Dislocated. Limbs pretending toward something I have no belief in. This work will not be like that. And you will fund it. It takes one woman because that is all it takes. No, she is not Jesus. I find the shape of the cross indexical: the crucifix— crosshatching. The cross imitates destination. You sign your name there, and this work is not about the individual. Yes, I already know the dancer. No, it's not nepotism. Try revenge. I am angry

because of the animals—so many animals cannot
fly. She should be able to fly. I take the bat as my
model. As for my audience—their eyes blank and
filled with sand—they offend me. Your questions
are meant to trip and humiliate and naked. You
think I lack grace. I do not. I will answer. Watch
the flashing stitch of my scalpel. It will answer—
it will connect us with blood.

[spoken from offstage right. six voices might alternate. one voice might do six.]

We have decided. You may propose. You've made notes on the cast?

I have. [blush. picks up papers. haltingly she.]

notes: on cast

one dancer

required to be omega
older than her peers, in some way
bird-like, quick and puckish, prone to flight
prone to spasms
prone to on-stage orgasm
armed with working feet and a hole
in her heart that could lead
to certain death (strains of the 5th—three duhs
one duhm) therefore

damaged
karma-wise, all birds have issues
hollow bones, a diet of seeds
small eyes, their alertness instinct
not intuition, not intellect although
appearing intellect, required to
required to fool us all—up to and including
moment omega, and crucially

she must not believe in her own death

[blush will. in all ways cringe before the six. speak.]

One cancer? Is this excision?
Is she a tumor, then, or a dove? Whom are you refusing peace?
What do you know of white? Blood? The microscopic prisons of the body?
How does one develop a personal symbolism? Does it come out of a series of apocalyptic
rejections?
By which system?
Was there a time when you thought, mistakenly, you were an artist?
And now?
Do you—your work—does it even have a title?

[shaky-papered.]

notes (2): title

I call it "sphinx"

—after all the animal forms, because as an adolescent
she wanted to be panther—before that
(we are told) the imagination
on a girl doesn't work, the lightbulb
unscrewed, pre-screwed
before fourteen the girl can only think (told
to think) princess movie-star princess ballerina princess
"sphinx" is the path any woman follows
to stone, and the setting out begins
at fourteen, or thereabouts, partly
because the woman chosen to dance this
has a body perpetually there
barely budded breasts, erratic menses (her neck
regrettably, reads twenty-nine) but
we have pancake, we have wigs
we have heavy heavy wings
the path to stone is long, like Job's, and this—
this happens to every woman who has ever wanted
as the world says no and no again and no
and her father says no and her mother, her aunts say no
and her sister glares at her from underneath, raging
that she has asked the unaskable,
which is—to have, or worse
that she may take

[blush is guilty. blush is guilty. blush is guilty. blush is guilty. blush is guilty. blush
is guilty. blush is guilty.]

We?

Sphinx?

notes (3): choreographer

[blush looks down. verifying.]

    is puppeteer
am puppeteer, I shouldn't mind
the cross
balsa wood with wires hanging
down, on the ends a woman
twitching
her last nerves
jangling, wind-
chiming—I shouldn't mind owning her
not owning my own body so clearly
she stands between me
and it, technically
dwarfing my own limbs—lengths
of clotted dust wrapped
inexpertly
around brief bones—(like asbestos
the warmth of glass disguised

as cotton candy)
my own limbs thud, truncated
things—while hers   extend
filled with blood and oil
capable of roll
and burn
and windmill—her whole body
working
what cannot be seen
into kinetics

                    while only my hand is employed

[blush traces two fingers through air. it is liminal. she is. distracted.]

                              Is this masturbation or possession?
                         Do you think you are a Gepetto? You are not.

                                        What he made lived.

[red. red how she stands. red the spot. red cyc. fist. foot. blush is red. call her red.]

          Do you want to see these? I can burn them. I have
          wanted to burn them. They are bag worms. They
          kill what they inhabit. Collectively, they are heavy
          as an albatross. Have you noticed?—so many
          white elements: every bird or bride a gravesite, a
          pupa. Wings are my deformities. I have too often
          stolen through these pages disturbing the air. You

asked to see them, you said you would consider,
and still you bait me as if I were your hook—
when what I am is fallen bits of sky tied up in
insect. You are gluttonous. Fish, fish—only
give me the space. I need a theater for my
death. And you have more than you have need.

Good. Reprimand us. It is what we ask for in a girl—moxie.
We are reminded—where will you hide the guillotine?
Death is larger than you think. Show us your notes on this.

notes (4): the set

[red gathers herself. a hand to her. dress. gathers its skirt. she holds it terse. terse
speaks.]

I dress the stage as
a single blade of grass
—sharp
so her feet bleed

have curtains hung
darkly—estranging
strangling her
between room and window

blindfolded
the set to her—a minefield

of opening
doors, dropped prosceniums

the audience directed
to stand and jeer, in masks
I sew, and place—
eyes out—on each stiff velvet seat

[red drops the dress. red hand on blush. the gathered slap.]

A seamstress too. You do everyone.
And what if she has hooves to feel no pain? Or what if night vision?
Nevertheless, we see it. You are hallucinogenic. Or visionary.
Now that we are rapt—score us. Use the knife.

notes (5): accompaniment

she will hear percussion
strings—

the heart and the heart, its two
reptilian chambers

Why not an orchestra?

any board of directors will
wonder why not an orchestra

her instability, I say, well-marked
by cello, bass and timpani
by high-hat and violin

by brush and pluck—pizzicato
undercut by static

or, alternately, sparse ivory—
a solo piano, the mind of the she (also
percussive, though less pleading, more
self-satisfied, more capable, not
of masturbation, but masturbation to climax
than string) spare
awkward-handed notes

this is a one-woman ballet
                              still
the board asks for a symphony
and perhaps a children's choir?
the community brought
together to fill seats
and promote a vast sleep
no Monk, no Pärt, no rock, no
computer music, original composition, local artist

if I must be avant-garde—why not Stravinsky—
soon, if not already, public domain?

Why not Stravinsky?

my answer is this
is a one-woman ballet
are you one woman?
am I? leave
me fucking alone

[Sigh.]   *What else?*

notes (6): lighting

the stage, side-lit from below—her face as if
just above a rising water—muscles outlined
in a reversal of shadow—the dancer semi-blind
and hobbled during each false exit—

she will know them

as shin-busters: the obstacles which light her way

And how do you know us?

[red looks offstage. the wing. the papers drop. the fingering. the curtain. the not.
mindlessly. the knotting up.]

The bored. Elite. Superior. Marrow-suckers,
melodramatists. Internal soliloquists. Those
who carry with them at all times the scent of
molding grain. Analysts. Aphids : cows of the
ant-world. Critics. Constipated money-releasers.
Excretionists. Snails—slow-moving and self-
fucking. Paternalistic, clever, correct. Faceless
and plural. Anemic. Undeniable. The chemical
cause of my paralysis—clothed in a gown of
strung teeth.

You flatter us.
We could tell you about ourselves. We must seem
to you—a swarm of immovables. Forested.

53

We are cannibals : this much fits. And
we are amused at your desire
to see yourself as zoo.
But scapegoating a thin likeness
is needless and typical. You might as well
cut out your daughter's clitoris and call it religion.

Now, tell us—will she wear a veil?

notes (7): costume

[pulling the curtain. coy. a cross her face. dropping. a smile almost. drops. to her knees. not a retrieve.]

the obvious choices are obvious and therefore
not available to me, being
as I am, for shock's sake
so I give Giselle the straight-jacket, drab
web edged in thorn to the sleeping
beauty, tatters
of sacrificial garb to any woman enough
to brave this write of spring

what is left is dross, dusty tapestries
of onions, scarves, polemics—

In lieu, what might you have her shed?

I would choose nakedness
were total vulnerability an option

it isn't——she must have
the illusion that she may yet
live through this, otherwise

her sour metallics and that look——
toward me and accusing——would
alert the audience to the punch-line

: she is about beauty about to die

I'll dress her in a leotard of bone
a cliché of porcelain
——shard, crescent, calla lily, moon——
the she: an electric white stone

(I am I suppose obvious)

that is its own shock, at least I pray
this is baroque——I am exhausted
of the minimal, and have for so long
longed to make something beautiful final

[red has undressed. awkward. naked. halting still. on knees. holds her dress out. into
the pit.]

Enough!
We were afraid we would be this
delighted by your technique.

You think us worms. Ahh.

notes (8): possible plot for Act 1

[as she reads. she stands. twists. as she twists. spins. the held dress drops. she is sometimes. spinning shattering. spot follows. good spot.]

fourteen   I will make it so that
the girl is on verge
of something, she can't
tell, the girl can't tell
what it is, nor
can she tell other things

cannot say happened   there is only no saying
happened is not her word
                              We can see your marginalia—did you want that?
dreamt is a word, imagined
is, purple is a bruise word
that gets green, spring is
get-green too, and green-getting—
that's envy, the girl has
an older sister who never tells
her anything   only body only

about older
they should be together
a force, instead
the girl is on
verge
without a railing, her sister
a vacant on the bed   one prop
lights out, as soft
as lead, do you think
the girl should write it down, or
should she smother it? she   a series of
does it   non-literal
with a pillow   duets
and it dies, she watches it—
the thing—
die

some things (not
the girl) have more
than that   end act one
one life though

[lights out. in black. six voices or one doing six repeat the following. 3 times. overlapping. eye of nude. or knot.]

You were an only child? A middle child? A squadron? We don't want the vague. The green. We want fashion. We want red is the new black. We want real fur again—we want leather. What happened to glamour? Who killed glamour? Was it your girl? Did you make her a killer? We do it out of love. Why did you do it? Did you tell her glamour was his belt-buckle? Did you hand her a knife? Did you tuck it discreetly under which pillow? The down one. Oh yes, the down...   When she left, dreaming homicide, what did she become? Is she Jesus? Are we supposed to buy that? Do not make us regret our investment. We could pull out, and then how hot is your bother? And into what pit might you let her fall? What would be her lowest rung? Give us a bite, pop culture or porn. Come on. Come all over.

notes (9): possible plot for Act 2

[lights on. red now not red. in a paper-white. a baccalaureate. red is white. call red white]

in the beginning of woman
nineteen, say, twenty-three
        movement throughout—stylized

woman has everything
woman has pearls and furs, a Jag
woman has men and education
woman has beauty and money enough to retain beauty
                              longer than is healthy or advisable?
woman wants no children
                    2-dimensional, hieroglyphic, flapper-esque
woman eats well, not
often, woman's appetite is relegated
to gin, amphetamines and sex—combinations
of these with furs and pearls
men, sometimes other
women   *Here we go*
women who don't own as much
woman is sad, as sad as other women, women
with children and food who are
sad, who don't have as much time
to eat themselves in quite the same way
                    deco, dancer angular, dancer arachnid
then woman
woman loses everything
read: a prodigal   *Old Testament*
unrepentant, unreturning, all
bone
dancer indecorous, exo-skeletal, emotion-ridden
a crying jag
years long, acres
woman does not find
inner strength, religion, a life-mate, irony
or purpose
                    given steps beyond virtuosity, dancer failing
woman shrivels

fat in her blood undermines
sanity   woman falls into a pit
lions in the pit, and she, lacking all and spine too
covets their furs and sharp pearls
their lumbar vertebrae, so
the woman takes on their hindquarters
and initiates "sphinx"   *Better*
                    more poise during descent, more poise, more
woman has not
woman has not yet
woman has yet to ask for anything
has yet to comprehend
encompass
                    dancer failing direction
woman, un-quixotic and un-faced
wildly, materially abandoned
woman outside the woman she never was inside
dancer passing from consciousness during second intermission
inside she never was woman, was, instead—
an erosion
                    brought back with salts

        by whom? —a sister?
of course, yes

[white picks up. waltzes papers in her paper-white. white is waltzing. whirls whitely.
falls. white. legs splayed. looks. like a doll. papers all over. all over her papers.]

                    Better, baby. Getting
                    rid of all that prurience—Now

—after the revival—
pull her plug and leave the little
bitch in the dark, okay?
yes, right
—there, there.

notes (11): solo—mad scene

[the six break into white speaking. white breaks rhythm never. allows them in spread-eagled. continues.]

they all go mad midway
through the white ballets and I
am somewhat a purist *the twist is if you—*
if I started her there
let her find touchstone
and had her lose it again her pain—
a purpling thing—like flowers
for a pet rat
her floor patterns
echoes of a mazed search for what
only fades
and at the end
some Pavlovian
reward maybe a lovely swan-death

she'd want to end it well

romantically she'd want me

to be sorry

unfortunate

that you—

that I do not factor—

as this is not a making

and having learned from previous studies

you will not be giving her

a name

—no

[six or one speak. as one.]

We think you have it, if you can just—

can you get to the end, sweets?

notes (12): possible plot for Act 3

[white speaks. pulling out her hair. pulling out lipstick. lipsticking. pulling out her lashes. pulling off. her dress again naked. pulling at her nipples. out her hair. again lipsticks. haltingly her. torso. pulling out her naked. her dead. she is dead. call her dead.]

choreographer enters stage left

I enter stage left

dancer is corpse

her half-body jutting out of stage right wing

she looks like a doll   *don't you think*
she looks like a doll?   I think
            the choreographer thinks
she looks like a doll
and it must have been a stabbing
            there is blood, the blue light
black shape
slowly transgressing the stage
as if the doll has a living, increasing
shadow
            as if an ocean were crossed
            on a bed
            and in the wake, a dark scar
the bed sits upstage
un-seaworthy, tall posters   *fire batons?*
—a gondola
through a narrow waterway at the entrance of ocean
and in this fake river, a floating
a girl, and the doll a girl doll, a Coppelia
no more bird riddling us with her
body   no dove released, no Ararat
no sands, no sphinx   *no more neon*
reading
            GOD—THIS WAY

only rats only scuttling beneath the stage
chute coal
            the blue light, black blood
diamond, something sharp, something cold
will be had from this
and not pearl, nothing
coats this with shimmering

the last theater riot ever

was never

over murder

        original, a success

        I bow   *you drop the knife*

the choreographer bows, drops the knife

my sister is dead

        I think *we think*

I think

a doll, a bird   a question

it is this:

        how could you kill us, angel? didn't you want us to be your mother?

[in an alley. torrential rodents

river ghastly silver from a stagedoor

some streetlamp barely capable

of offering them   out

dead bows six times. stage right. dead bows once into the pit. dead drops her
lipstick. the lipstick rolls. down the raked stage. cellist and drummer stand. both
bow deep to dead. deep. deep from the waste.]

3

Not me. Not that. But not nothing, either.
—*Julia Kristeva*

ANGEL, BOXED: A POETICS

To fit, disarticulate. Angels are coherence intensified to the point immediately prior to the point (non-dimensional) of god's face. If hacking, if pieces are no option, can an angel be contorted into box? Can you fold a blue flame? A sword? Or would that preclude genocide, retribution—be "unnatural"? Angels have no nature, existing as a midway. A path between the freakish but not a dharma, as you cannot ride one. On the left, freakishuman—on the right, freakish gulf where all freakish was once engulfed. How then to cube an angel? Frieze. They are stone fish anyway. I don't like them. Anything you do to get the angel in the box is acceptable. Is poem. Make them crystalline. No, don't. The shatter trope's too democratic, too a little bit for everyone, too through a glasnost sharply. Acid then. Yes, immerse an angel in chemistry. A set piece. Sublimation. Do not let the angel pass through liquid. Do not let the angel make water. Interrogate. Collect her steam in a red balloon. Box the balloon.

O DEAREST, DEAREST B.

It is purple, a day about lettuce. A day to get
the grief across. I open the corpse
with a letter opener. Clay
moons that tug at the corners give way.
The thing about ceramics is: ovens.

How very unwilling you were
to consider sleeplessness. But like it—
I could have been a valid indicator of my emotions.

The space at the back of the jaw is the House of Sorrow.
When the woman I go to gets to my face
it is there she places her thumbs to hurt me.

After sex we'd open
the refrigerator because it was late. Bright
bright packaging would hum and quarrel. Eat me! No! Eat me!
But this would last less than a minute.

Bonaparte, you'd say. What you meant
was that I should not make any more phone calls.
I don't trust the housework, and I don't
the in-ground pools. Not anymore.
When I told you about the radio, you waved
an aluminum bat warning three times past my head.

Everybody knows. You. Couldn't. Hit.
I braced against but you put down the violence.
I went out into the garden.

I sowed, on the third Wednesday after
the Bermuda grass came back—*Agate* and *Perpetua*.

And on the morning of the new moon after that—
Heartblind and *Hemsong*. Two days later
I slit the ground like tinfoil for *Silverflecked Antestes*
and the following night at half-past eleven
I interred you, *Boris*, who were my husband.

Despite the murder—will this be another one you win?
This time, from under the yard.

I will never rid the house of blackflies.
The girls grow big without you. Girls
we never had.

The bone-juggler tossed his hard
scarves against air. Someone's

parts in rearrangement. Not all parts.
Some go before. Some are boiled

away and then there's lye.

This one woman had no uterus.
None ever do. She was his

newest bones. Done parsing her
out by weight into the others'

piles of birch—

the bone-juggler makes a recipe
and stuffs the proper sacks in

preparation—as I might
several birds for a wedding.

WRITING SPIDER (FOR BOURGEOIS)

i

The spider is a novelist.

ii

Liar.

The spider's knitting-needle gams are not a knitter's gams.
The spider is a shiny-black beauty machine.
A revolver.
A liar lying. Relying. Killing.

The spider is predictably a woman
and someone wrote "by Bourgeois, rehabilitated as maternal."
So. They have succeeded in turning the whore
at the ankles.

iii

It takes thirteen men to screw in a spider.
That is, I have learned, the line of custody for the execution.
Exhibition. Sometimes a lesser guard
falters because of her beauty.
Sprain.
He is not culpable.

iiii

When I fall for a spider I do not say she seduced me.
I say the tuffet was slippery, sun got caught in my eyes.

iiiii

The spider is Wolf-Spider—a hyphenate, a ululate.
A lone.
The spider might have a child or a thousand, but that is hardly the point.
She has no pack. The point is her end-machine.

A home woven by circling for kill.

There, there now, torture. Don't fret.
When you are torture, the spider is almost always your mother.
The liquefaction of prey—
ink.

iiiiii

I will not discuss here the nature of a spider's secretions.
How silk cuts. Lies against itself.
Suspended steel snaps, flies apart. A bridge plummets
lashing into unwitting suicides.
Virgules.
I will not describe here
how the slits left in the dew resemble vaginas.
There is a death too at the center of you.
A tiny swinging expiration and you are failing
trapeze, clock, an end-breath drawn—only to be sipped into her
like a moan.

iiiiiii

She knits wounds.
Each day a new one of a thousand like oubliettes.

These are her infants. Threaded
things, traps.

Call this monster.

I do not doubt spiderlessness is also a virtue.
Some women touch babies in public who are not touched
enough privately. Scavenge
babies. It is only another alternative.

Say that.

Say I have not been touched enough privately.
But you are too smart for self-pity.
Kindness.
You pick up these long skewers.

iiiiiiii

To have written the spider.
To have crushed her to asterisk. At the bottom of the page
it would read, *See interview with the poet/sculptor/felon—Appendix A.*
Instead, I lie inside the figure.
I try on spider.
It is all I feel can be done—persuasively—with a mother.

MARRIAGE (2)

In the bent city
we tip over from too much standing.
You stand for father.
I attempt to stand-in for the protagonist
who's gone into hiding.
We've wrapped our arms around the dead
like a rug to carry them to the dumpster.
We're that kind and the dead are up too many flights.
You jimmy locks while I offer readings
and we make just enough
to pretend.
On weekdays bills knock about
the insides of walls we don't own.
We don't pay
and the dead get louder.
Sometimes there are children across the street in a lot.
You throw bottles down at the asphalt
and talk about the colors.
Really, you want them to cut each other up—
so I won't want one.
That night, we ask each other whose turn it is in bed.
You say the hungrier one should cook
so I cook.
The dead make everything taste like caraway.
When I spit into the sink there is blood and this
is the beginning of what you can't give.
You are much older than I am.
I am young enough to hate the dead.

When the ostrich is removed from its feathers—the black, the gray-white plumes—they are filthy. Fine, ecstatic combs have been constructed. The grime must be painstakingly attracted, and then raked out. The combs go through over and over so that, eventually, it cannot be counted. Children do this. It becomes as if the feathers have never skimmed across grasses, baked and sharp. Never flightlessly rummaged the plains. Once, ostriches were looking for enough wind. After an ostrich has been removed from its feathers, asking belongs to other birds. But the wind in hiding stays close to the ground. Sometimes the wind goes under. The children combing have been known to come upon it in the depths of their fingers. It is their secret rheumatism—and they hoard it like a bread.

MAIDEN MEAD

It was when September, ending
jealous, eats bees. We

nervoused again for the island
in a boat still made of rocking.

With bees follow-
ing. In fluid zum,

oar-sweeping rhythms of dip
and churn: driblets of bees, bees

as sung humidity—condensed
over wings of boat. Above

lake we did not hurry, bee and boat
were dim punishers, chiders or nuns

of it: the keeping on.
Wore we shushing cages

and veiled we eyes with mesh,
or fingers kittening? None

of it. We, trembly and suspect, eyed
the sun hung over water like comb

dripping out just how a woman wants
bees. Summer fermented, parted lake hair—

and in bee spillage—took
our island. And though

we had been in terror brave—we were made
nebulous, voices hid amidst a hymn of dying

drunken bride. This, now, is how
we say to see it: bees eaten.

BAD NIGHT, BAD

Each star hangs
on a separate bolt of silk and by a different name
claims the universe.

I have never been so much a reptile.

A mother inside
a Matchbox
drives her son's hand across linoleum.

Unable to sleep—she tosses
others from sleep.

Dreams
are narcotic—and should be
remastered before a next batch
kills.

Nothing doing nothing.

That's what's wrong with
3 AM. 4 AM has other priorities,
gambits. Gothams.

4 AM can kid itself
it's morning. Though that's

just the birds.

GALLERY OF THE DAUGHTER

after Man Ray

Theatre

I can't talk to you
about the archangel. She said.
We sank even further down into the worn velvet-esques.
She whispered under the soundtrack of the re-release. She said
I'd give a thousand dollars to see him fly.
She didn't have anything like that
on her. She was sunburnt all around her spaghetti straps
and she spat a little when she recounted a vision
because she hurried.

The rope dancer accompanies herself with shadows

You might think this is about
the circus. You would call it an allegory.
What if rope means pills? What if dancer
is mother? I've had some success with numbers
up until now. I could tell you 9 and 17,
then 22, then 38 and already in, out
of hospitals a decade. What would you
make of it? You should know
she was loving. No one asks that.

Dancer (Danger)

Tremendous. The oak's height
and the sturdy make of branches it offered up
to climbing novices. When we walked by the cloister
on the way to the bus-stop she would
squeeze my hand and say how sorry she was
for that poor tall boy, locked behind
stone with thirty doddering goddies.

The twenty days and nights of Juliet

Let's just say
the first time she left
I was unprepared for her turmoil of return.

Coatstand

That event deserves another go.

She got on a bus into the Midwest and woke
two and a half weeks later in a motel in Dubuke
in somebody else's clothes. She had her wallet,
a blond wig, and menthol cigarettes
she started smoking then and
for the next five years.

Policemen brought her home
filthy. The doorbell
woke me, I was not old enough yet
not to be sleeping well.
I held somebody's gnarled rabbit-fur stole
for an hour while she made and drank her own tea.

Indestructible Object

That would be her daughter.
That would be me. I am her daughter.
I am a liar. That would be her daughter.
That would be a lie. I would be her daughter.
If she would have had a daughter, I would be
that daughter. No, that
would be a lie. In truth I am
a march of lies.

P O S I T I O N A L

the candy was in the milk
and on the first day
you strained yourself for it
through the cervix

your heart is now
in the refrigerator next to the olives
a chart there calculates
what you are capable of

the boy you loved is inside
the girl you hate
often, irrevocably

the table is in the chair

the chair is in the plan
the floor inside the lantern
influenza is in the syringe
winter—inside the flowers

this may serve furious
but you deal yourself cards
and play toward anyway

the statues are in the water
swimming   the Coliseum
in a fishbowl

the fish are in a basket
they are dead   but don't
get maudlin, they were fish

the book is in the thing
the thing in the market
the market, inside world history

world history is inside
the prison you are free
to move about   laugh here

beyond this—the eye swaddled
in glass
dreams fracture, no?

DEPOSITION

I led the accused out from a wing onto the field of inquiry. Because it was my first time I forgot the proper footing. The accused comforted me, saying, "we could sing."

When I recited the allegory of the potsticker then asked the accused to supply meat, it was as if something had fallen in. A sole from the foot of a hanged woman. Ceremoniously, we wet our mouths with citrus. The judge looked on, then signaled my adequacy.

I took my seat among jurors.

A small woman urged me to confess. I sat at the corner. A man who was sick wanted me to relieve his bowels. But it was not my turn for nurse.

We were some of us left in the dark to show others the way back.

The judge's behaviors were scandalous. The batting of eyelashes and adjusting of handicaps. The getting low on great knees. The most travestied material wrung out and reapplied with lard.

Up in the balcony, we played solitaire in our woolens. The fires were elsewhere. Divorced from certain tenets of enlightenment, we could recognize no moral disorders. Most of us didn't care to try the accused, but that wouldn't stand during sentencing.

During sentencing we'd have to invent a new horror to accompany each stricken, each damage, each unknowing decency.

I was elected foreman as I'd been named jailor, court reporter. The rest averted their good eye. I had been absent during the accused's childhood. I would eventually fail to evade the consequences.

Currently, the other jurors wanted nothing more than to be told. It was a large and severe want.

The judge left instructions. Footprints in the conference room were set in a Viennese waltz. We took turns counting each other out in threes. Each time, someone had to keep time while others were made to touch. Most did what they could dully.

When reminded of gravity and of our homes, we collapsed one by one into a single volume. We walked out like children who have cheated or been caught in each other's underclothes. I thought very hard about small, about seeds and pits and pollen. I listened for an oboe.

After it was done, I was not there.

After it was done, the accused pale clay on a metal field, it was done. It went as expected: priest, needles, death-rattle, curtain. I drove slowly home in the leftover quiet planning a soup.

Black Johannes thinks every tiny
a fetish—*Tell me how that makes
them wrong*. In aisle 4
produce offers wax
and cheerless pushes against
horror, abutting it. In hardware
rows of drawers teem
with machine tinies. Here a twist.
There, what and puncture. Screws,
squirrels, buried nails. A hopeful feel
that things could still be welded
together or caged—ignoring rot
or given a year, or sawdust.
*Is dry, operatic room-sized death better
death?* Me—mine is
green eyes shot
out a fist of shrunken
potato. O my head, my
head. My moan flower.

1.

The song weeps because this one child was never born.

           There were other children; there were even girls. None were her.
After she was not born, she became my tree-frog, my wisdom on the terrace, as her
uncle was before her.

                   She had that liberty.
(I would say *come, dancer*. And she would not come. That kind of liberty.)
   She was not owned. She did not fit in a mind-furrow or pocketbook. She did not
            want to fit. Even as an empty breath, she held herself blue.
In that way, you might think *ahh, the poet*. Well, that's laughable.
    Ferocity, her aunt. Her grandmother, ocean. She might have been something.
   Genetically speaking, female is our default. She was my daughter because she was
                   not at all.
In May, spring comes to its first close. The fans come on, slicing.

2-4.

        Somewhere in this gap I had her laughing.

5.

Shadowgirls shouldn't have such full lives, literarily.
    It's harder to pity them. I do a disservice to the genre, giving her mirth.

6.

You want to think of her with her face behind a sheer in a pre-dawn sort of milieu. I
know it.

       What if I gave her a graveyard in the mid-west? A discolored monument in the
             shape of a worried saint? No. Cymbals crash. It's that kind of song.
So, how to write her out. She's cursive, at least. I know that. Not to lift the pencil up,
I mean.

       And she's green. That's in her name. She's careful, on steps and in crowds. In
           crowds, there are so many just like her. But she keeps to me.

7.

I need your hands   is what she
says.

8.

My other child doesn't know her. She knows him. She does little things like muss his
hair as he sleeps.

      Harmonious. That's how I'd call it. Contrapuntal. She is a chord. The left hand,
        except in rags. If he still played piano, my husband might be able to see.

9.

In the hospital—a picture of a zebra. On my 25th St. Patrick's Day, I dyed my hair
white and tattooed the word *dark* on my ass—markings I chose out of some spite.

         My life, my life, mine. A sick mirage, shabby, lasting too long.
Shatter. No mirror offered itself as inane but punctual omen. One should have.
Enough of them at the time, ceiling to floor. Me using them to perfect a body.

            A body without other considerations.

10.

Note: Houses have too many walls.

Ones that keep the outside out, ones that keep the inside in pieces.

11.

Dance class. I came home. At eight, the age. I said, *I don't have the body for this.*

Do you want to quit?   *No.*

I mean to be my mother's daughter. To be that, it involves suffering.

I could have studied painting. Except I was after articulation. I was after revelation.

After apocalypse, clearly a dancing thing.

I remember the end of the world, come and come again. It took a full year, the year between millennia. I crossed it like a tundra.

The core grows fiercer as the self is edited. Clippings. Straight black hairs in the bathtub.

Centuries of inches.

Shorter. No, just above the shoulders; you still have to pull it up.

And then I shaved it.

12.

My mother's daughter should never want to be so—well—so unattractive.

She liked it white, my mother did, brittle as icing.

13.

What she is, is ghost. As contrary and/or pliant as any weed, any daughter, any brush untangling.

14.
Could my son have begun (rather than if he will end) life as a haunting:

       —presence, an odor of lilac on the back staircase. flicker. the normal
                shifts in temperature.
   sudden, internal wind. shudder of motherhood.
   cold, ripe
        then   as quickly as: the house was un-empty
  it is not——   —again
    the child, doubly down, manifesting now, only within the walls of its
             mother
   the actual house clear   a year   nearly
   to wait   (in open waiting
       in quiet waiting)
     for bright
   full return
               —but this
this is lullaby—my son, never so frail a terror.
       She began as haunting and there remains.

15.
What I can see of her, from here, is all limb.
Four-pointed star. North star, not true north. North pole—not the actual north pole,
        but convenient facsimile.
If she is there, up, she is both star and black place that actual star resides, which may
or may not be in the direction of the perceived star.
      Gravity bends light: she is heavy as locked doors.
The long-locked-in hair of stars. Hair: part of us that died.

16.

Ad/Omissions:

My mother was—not why I danced.
   To feel ice-flecked wind on scalp skin, was only the one reason to move. To fly. To
steal from/against. A different steel.
Tested mettle. Necessary to say "love" to say "son" every day. A different sun. Not
anyone's business. The weather of love arrives, troubling, during the short days.
And so etches.
I do not *say* to her. She is not beyond winter. I do not say these things. These things
I am saying.

17.

Sage. Something weights still in me. A lead plumb at the pit, the red open space
at the top of my cervix.
   With each child, mother is diminished. No one tells you this. Or how you will bleed.

18.

Oughtn't I to leave it go? This diabolical umbilicus, kite string sans, get to spring,
get there.
Just get.
What I know is what was unexpected.
I scrape out space for her and have more.

THE YOUNG HYSTERECTOMY RECOGNIZES THE SHAPE OF HER MOUTH

When the old mother eats me I am the old mother. I wear her long black doula skirts with pockets to Rangoon. Underneath, my thighs drip split berry juice. The wrong berries. The wrong wet. When I wake I am the old mother spider in a white room where they have shaken sparks from my crochet. The young at my feet tell me I am not over. Their faces are washers. Their faces are eggs and nuts. What will happen to them when suddenly death? I ask them to turn away while I rub blood into what is cold. They do not change color. It is the old mother who cracks up opening her shoe, her cupboard, the long corridor on the tenth floor. Cold and flickering light was an idea she had about a bird skeleton. I do not ask which bird. Had I been baba, my ideas would've been brandy. We eat at an empty table. I stove shockings into my mouth until they run in currents down my chin. The old mother and I have lost our teeth in the soup. Like the last of the sweet, the electric corn, this—smacking its lips of winter.

ORPHANAGE: A PASTORAL

In the meadow of rotting children
stood a boy taller than the others.
Maybe he had not been so long dead.
I looked into the swarming
caviar of his eyes, and saw in the moving black
warnings, the archives of the field: One girl
had been returned because
she was inside-out. Her skin
was inside-out, and she stained everything.
One boy was prickly,
and cactuses—it was noted
there—in the sockets—

                go unloved.
There were two
who might've been catching. Four
attached at the tongue, faces atwist
in a perpetual corner of sibling. The list
went on. I extended a hand and thumbed
down the tissue-thin lids (one tore) and hummed
modestly along with the flesh-drunk flies
as my feet sank into the earth, my eyes—
like his: in static witness: fields.

DUTIFUL, THE SISTER

for my godmother

She was not heavy—my sister. The burlesque
is when you open her to find the composition entirely chain.

What happened was the sea. Let the sea stand in for death.
Faith. She approached the sea reluctantly, but could not acquiesce.

And spinning herself gold
and walking away, each step more cumbersome than the last,

she was an open glove, fingers darned with bleeding.
Her bones, how light they had been.

She walked curtain after curtain to links, shifting, gaining gravity—
also she was less substantial. All of her

was only there to hold herself together. Hands, hands, more hands.
If she were paper, she would be dolled, holding her own, almost infinitely.

It might be this, to be a ghost, to be unprotected by the body, to must
touch reality, a tongue, at the very least—others.

She was not waspish—she sought not. She asked me to lift her—
she was a series of perfect o's—to take her somewhere green.

She was mail, even if you call them months, or mouths.
Even if you could pierce her, and I could not. She was

unstung. If only: a hatpin. If only
I could hold her, and carry her as a father would.

When I let her go, she stopped asking for me to let her go.
I laid her down between thick roots and waited for her

to disappear upwards, taking cover in leaves.
She folded down, letting leaves cover her, more armor.

We passed autumn that way, staring into each other,
her face gnawing away at itself.

Can you want your heart to die? I wanted
that. Rather than keeping her as she was keeping—

leatherbark, eroded cropland. What there
held in place by dead root and ethic.

Or by metal—a sick color—the sea not the sea.
Take it that I trust faith not. Beautiful word.

I played at, no—   *was*
the dutiful sister ever failing.

Fail.   Now—
there's a beautiful name for a girl.

In artistry and largess, rearrange them.
In anger, they are to be arranged, re-
arranged, then done again. They are angels—
rearrange them. They are disastrous. They will
resist. Yet, do not cease. Glacial
in their garments, regal in glades and groves,

in dense grasses—distressful—
as they, in-inebriate, sling back sober growlers
of lager, or indifferently wrangle geraniums
into itty pots, better at to tend
and to protect than obstetric nurses
are, or prostitutes heeled precariously above

loved window boxes—rearrange them.
Their glands and ovaries. Make their knotless
hearts bear the pendulous weight of
bowels. Make them start
to resemble humanity. Deform them
with anatomy. Given the difficulty of insides,

they would not be so aether. Flawlessness
is mere, a porcelain mug in which such
unbearabilities steep: terrible
symmetry and so forth. It is time
they were not right. It is time they were
treated to the vast interior they lack.

Next to the sofa—sit the wingback, float
the ottoman in front of puddled drapes.
Curl up inside an angel: be

the fetus. In this way, they
could be made to matter. Off heads
of pins, not new age schtick, no longer

beads on philosophical abaci, nor tendrils
withering in the schizophrenic mind
—but bodied. So they may truly be
ours and us theirs, we'd say. All the while
we'd know—bothered not—the translation
into mother to be exaltation. Murder, also.

ABOUT THE AUTHOR

KIRSTEN KASCHOCK was the second, and then the third, of five children. She has degrees from Yale University, the University of Iowa, and Syracuse University. She earned her Ph.D. in English from the University of Georgia. Kirsten is currently a doctoral fellow in dance at Temple University. Her first book of poetry, *Unfathoms*, is available from Slope Editions. She resides in Philadelphia, Pennsylvania, where she likes to make things, and sometimes people.

Ahsahta Press

Ahsahta Press

NEW SERIES

MODERN AND CONTEMPORARY POETS OF THE AMERICAN WEST SERIES

Many of the books in this series are available for download at
http://scholarworks.boisestate.edu/ahsahta/

This book is set in Apollo MT type with Titling Gothic FB Normal titles
by Ahsahta Press at Boise State University
and manufactured by Thomson-Shore, Inc.
Cover design by Quemadura.
Book design by Janet Holmes.

AHSAHTA PRESS

2011

JANET HOLMES, DIRECTOR
JODI CHILSON, MANAGING EDITOR

KAT COE

CHRIS CRAWFORD

TIMOTHY DAVIS

CHARLES GABEL

KATE HOLLAND

GENNA KOHLHARDT

BREONNA KRAFFT

MATT TRUSLOW

ZACH VESPER

EVAN WESTERFIELD